YOUR KNOWLEDGE HAS VALUE

- We will publish your bachelor's and master's thesis, essays and papers

- Your own eBook and book - sold worldwide in all relevant shops

- Earn money with each sale

Upload your text at www.GRIN.com and publish for free

Individualism in the 21st Century. Why Communication Became Impossible

Lisa Thöne

Bibliographic information published by the German National Library:

The German National Library lists this publication in the National Bibliography; detailed bibliographic data are available on the Internet at http://dnb.dnb.de.

ISBN: 9783389028810
This book is also available as an ebook.

© GRIN Publishing GmbH
Trappentreustraße 1
80339 München

Print and binding: Books on Demand GmbH, Norderstedt, Germany
Printed on acid-free paper from responsible sources.

GRIN web shop: https://www.grin.com/document/1477007

University of Paderborn
Department of English and American Studies
Winter Term 2018/19
Seminar: Individualism and Culture

Individualism in the 21st Century
Why Communication Became Impossible

Lisa Thöne

Englischsprachige Literatur und Kultur
und Englische Sprachwissenschaft

Table of Contents

> Listening effectively to others can be the most fundamental and powerful communication tool of all. When someone is willing to stop talking or thinking and begin truly listening to others, all of their interactions become easier, and communication problems are all but eliminated (Johnson qtdn. Way).

Ken Johnson referred to individualism in an extreme form when indirectly hinting to people who do not listen to others. In such an extreme condition, no one sees the need to listen to anybody but themselves. So, can communication properly exist if no one listens and can oneself even fulfill one's own dreams and wishes without interaction with other people? The answer seems to be clear: If no one listens, life must look much harder and unfulfilled. However, is that a condition so apart from the current 21st Century? When having a look at Social media, where everyone is promoting oneself in an extensive way, few people seem to truly listen to others than themselves and this topic is also what the singer Aaron Weiss processes in certain songs from his band *mewithoutYou's* album *Catch For Us The Foxes*. Out of this reason, these songs form the primary source for this paper.

The aim of the research conducted in this paper is to prove that communication in the 21st Century became almost impossible due to the focus on sending as a means of expressing one's own individualism, which causes mental and social issues.

As a first step, the band *mewithoutYou* and their album *Catch For Us The Foxes*, which contains the primary sources, will be presented to gain a general understanding of who the band is and what the relevance of this particular album is for the broader context of this paper. Subsequently, the reader will get an overview of the individualism in the 21st Century and to complete the background/theory chapter, it will be explained how communication works and what happens if it does not work because communication problems will play an important role in the course of this paper.

In the analysis, the singer Aaron Weiss' former self-promotion will be examined to then draw a line to the Social media usage nowadays. After this, his critique and way out will be considered in detail. As the last step of the analysis, consequences of too much focus on oneself will be mentioned, including social and various mental health issues, which can arise through this.

Finally, all findings will be summed up, the thesis statement will be taken into account again, and it will be named what kinds of further research could be done.

In order to analyse the significance of the depicted lyrics from the band mewithoutYou's album *Catch For Us The Foxes,* it is necessary to gain a general understanding of who this band and the story behind their album is (cf. "MewithoutYou").

MewithoutYou "consists of vocalist Aaron Weiss, guitarist Michael Weiss and Brandon Beaver, bassist Greg Jehanian, and drummer Rickie Mazzotta" ("MewithoutYou"). They come from America, Philadelphia in Pennsylvania. The genre of the band can be described as *rock*, whereby it contains "spoken-word vocals and free ranging drums, bass and guitar" ("MewithoutYou"). Aaron Weiss, who was part of another band before, formed *mewithoutYou* in 2000 because of his passion for experimenting (cf. "MewithoutYou"). To portray a contrast to the formerly harsher music, the name MewithoutYou was chosen for this group, but despite the contrast it fitted (cf. E. Tommy). The band has released seven albums from 2000 to 2018 (cf. "MewithoutYou").

Catch For Us The Foxes is their second album and was released in 2004 (cf. "MewithoutYou"). During the creation of it the band had a hard time because it was made with much effort and consideration (cf. Harrison 105). However, Paul Matthew Harrison, a friend of Aaron Weiss, emphasized that "Aaron's style made the band unique" (105). As he did not find himself in a healthy mental state at that time, Aaron wrote the songs with a lot of hope and processed many thoughts in the writing process (cf. Harrison 107). It was at that time that the vocalist began dressing in clothes from "dumpsters and thrift stores" and "eating almost exclusively from the trash" (111). Also, his values became clearer: They were "Christian values, not leftist values" as he was concerned about religion (113). Aaron incorporated many beliefs and philosophical thinkers but also criticized many beliefs and belief systems (cf. Harrison 113).

To depict the circumstances of extreme individualism in the 21st Century, Monbiot has offered a thorough explanation that seeks a general understanding of problems which arise during that time and their main reasons (Monbiot).

For every age there is a certain designation, but the recent age is not defined when it comes to society (cf. Monbiot 9). Monbiot's approach to define it is to call it the "*Age of Loneliness*" (ibid.). Thus, he claims that the society has become highly individualistic.

Subsequently, he detects an issue. Humans have always lived together and had to align their lives in dependence which is a problem when they do not do so anylonger and must cause not only mental but also social issues (cf. Monbiot 9-10). This is underlined as he states loneliness to be a disease (cf. Monbiot 10). Isolating oneself enhances circumstances like "dementia, high blood pressure [and] alcoholism" (ibid.). The reason for isolation is explained through the concepts of "*individualism and competition*", which receive a lot of attention in society (cf. ibid.). What can be derived from this is that those concepts are recently not perceived as a problem for humans nor for society. Additionally, Monbiot mentions that not only surveys prove that but also the language as humans address others as "*loser[s]*", "*individuals*" and use the phrase "*personally speaking*" to express their own desires and point of views (10-1).

Then the author moves on to describe the *television* as a medium which is on the one hand used by people who want to escape isolation but on the other hand they get dissatisfied with what they have watching more successful people (cf. Monbiot 11-2). It is clearly shown that technology can radicalise this entanglement of individualism and loneliness.

Monbiot deduces and proves that in the current age humans cannot be happy, not even through wealth (cf. Monbiot 12). People themselves are no longer satisfied and also lost connections to one another (cf. 12-3). As a solution the social system must be changed (cf. 13). Finally, he concludes that the lives "are becoming nasty, brutish and long" (ibid.).

By the hands of communication humans are capable of imagining different concepts (cf. Burgoon et al.). They can express their thoughts, thus their individualism, due to their ability to produce speech signals (cf. ibid.). Lives and minds are built up through these proceedings because understanding begins by listening to other persons (cf. ibid.). However, an interaction between people can be led by manipulation of one participant for the sake of the other one's own satisfaction and pleasure (cf. ibid.). The more lies are being spread, the trickier it gets to comprehend complex structures of the world and even to listen to others in order to do so (cf. ibid.). The trust is broken and humans isolate themselves from specific views and even from other people (cf. ibid.).

Communication has certain properties, which can be observed. The people who are interacting choose the time the interaction shall find its ending, thus it is dependent on individual circumstances and on the communicating subjects (cf. Burgoon et al. 11). This also entails that no communication can ever look exactly the same (cf. Burgoon et al. 14). Nevertheless, that does not mean that the communicating subjects have total control over their communication, how and which goal shall be achieved (Burgoon et al. 18). Moreover, it is possible that the whole communication can be led into a new direction if one issue gets altered (cf. Burgoon et al. 12).

In addition to those properties of communication, four different scenarios exist according to Burgoon et al.: If the "[s]ource has an intent to communicate and the "[r]eceiver perceives an intent to communicate" too, communication happens (Burgoon et al. 21). Vice versa, if neither the "[s]ource [nor the] receiver [have or perceive any] intent to communicate", *behavior* replaces communication (ibid.). A different scenario can be observed when the "[s]ource does not have an intent to communicate" but the "[r]eceiver perceives an intent to communicate" (ibid.). Then, Burgoon et al. describe the scenario as "[a]scribed communication" (ibid.). Lastly, the fourth scenario is that the "[s]ource has an intent to communicate" but the "[r]eceiver does not perceive any attempt to communicate", which is called a "communication attempt" (ibid.).

Stuart Hall developed a similar idea when referring to the terms "*encoding*" and "*decoding*" (Hall). What he means by these terms is that every message gets encoded by the sender and decoded by the receiver, so that the message that the receiver gets, can be interpreted greatly different, even in a contradictory manner as it was intended by the sender (Hall).

Due to the mentioned aspects, problems in the communication process occur rather frequently. They can either develop out of less consideration before making a propostion, or out of less consideration when decoding the received message (Burgoon et al. 22; Hall).

Problems of communication lead to conflicts, which have to be solved. Those conflicts can be approached differently by individuals (cf. Burgoon et al. 343). Avoiding to cope with a present conflict causes an accumulation of problems that at some later time can become suffocating to the individual (cf. ibid. 343). On the other hand, a conflict can be handled in an accommodating style which means to value other's needs higher than one's own needs to solve conflicts quickly and with great attention to other person's well-being (cf. ibid. 343-4). A competition can be found when people do not want to confess their own fault for the conflict, whereas a compromise is a *balanced situation* where everyone plays an equal part (cf. ibid. 344-5). If this is taken further, the participants in the conflict work together in order to manage the conflict and to consequently solve it (cf. ibid. 345).

Generally, there is not much information given about Aaron Weiss' mindset concerning his lifestyle before he inverted everything. Despite that, through mewithoutYou's song texts, he metaphorically offers an insight but it was not until a certain point in time that he figured out what Christianity really meant to him and what he expected it to be (cf. E., Tommy). When he sings about the "*Shining One*" in him, Aaron means something god-like, or something positive that remains inside of him ("Leaf"). Furthermore, he wishes to "become the servant of all", which refers to a biblical verse, so it portrays his religious view-point ("January 1979").

Another hint to his lifestyle before the change can be found in an entry he made about himself during that time. The singer describes how he was living in a rather dependent that independent manner with his parents at the age of 25 (cf. Harrison 78-9). The singer's wish to "become the servant of all" could thus be related also to his relationship with his parents at the age of 25 because at that time, they did everything in the household for their son and now Aaron wants to give them back what they once did for him and reverse situations ("January 1979"). Nonetheless, not only did he demonstrate less responsibility towards his parents but also towards a girl and Jesus as he describes it as a person concerned about religion (cf. Harrison 78-9). The text passage "[m]y forehead no longer sweet [w]ith holy kisses" could indicate on the girl he let down because of his selfish behavior or to his mother ("January 1979"). Regardless of his feelings of guilt and his wish "to want one thing", which is "the purity of heart", he changed nothing (cf. Harrison 78-9). The repetitions of this wish in his singing let the exclamation seem like a call for help. So far, it can be summarized that he acted out of individual self-interest, did not listen to others and was polarized by that. In the song "*Leaf*" Aaron Weiss sings

> Well, I was charming you at best […]
> But if you stay up too late
> I'll throw you back into the cupboard
> With all the chipped and dirty plates
> Like the carnival game with the bottleneck and rubber ring…
> Where even if you win
> Even then you don't win ("Leaf").

Through these lines he admits that he talks to his fans and expresses that he didn't want to have a deep relationship with people, he rejects deep conversations and if a point of view does not fit his own he cancels the conversation ("Leaf"). Referring to the carnival game, Aaron could have meant that when only accepting point of views compliant with one' own, the counterpart makes a claim, metaphorically throwing the rubber ring, which does not have an effect. The singer seduced people to admire him but that was not an act anybody gained anything from because it is not a mutual relationship but rather a onesided speaking from Aaron's side, which hinders him on caring about others and enriching his world-view through a different perspective taking ("Leaf"). Those particular findings can also be derived from other passages in the song *Leaf*.

Clearly, Aaron Weiss' former behavior can be discovered in various forms of 21st Century Social media. Just like him willing to make fans admire him for spectacular presentations on stage, many young people on the social media platform *Instagram* also point to highly individualistic and self-promoting behavior when they present their seemingly happy lives and products that viewers yearn for (cf. Khamis et al. 191). It can be derived that the so called *influencer* communicates with the viewer by showing him a certain way of life combined with a matching product which could facilitate the viewer to achieve this lifestyle (cf. ibid.). That is known as "*self-branding*" (cf. ibid.). The same onesided communication like between Aaron and his fans can be observed since both contrasted persons, the influencer and Aaron, are solicitous in promoting themselves.

Often, the sending of individual concerns and wishes is taken so far that the individual wants to convert others for the sake of fulfilling one's own ideology (Harrison 130). Aaron Weiss criticizes that such a compulsion towards people does not have anything to do with loving and serving them and thus to place oneself on the same level with others (cf. ibid.). In the song "Leaf", the singer puts it into other words when claiming

> However much you talk…
> However well you talk
> You make a certain sense
> But still it's only stupid talk
> However much I strut around…
> However loud I sing
> The shining One inside me won't say anything ("Leaf")[.]

This involves that other individuals can be hardly converted through neither a huge amount of talking nor by a high volume as long as the quality of the talking does not have an impact on the receiver and thus also the sender does not obtain anything.

Yet, the entanglement is enlarged by the use of Social media (cf. Turkle). Technology pretty much enforces the individual to focus only on the own interest and point of views (cf. ibid.). When for instance sitting at the table together as a family, it is possible to only *pretend* to listen to others (cf. ibid.). A great problem arises if this situation is transferred onto the situation of being at a funeral because then feelings of "grief [...] [and] revery" are not fully permitted (ibid.). Certainly, that shows that not only one another's views can be easily neglected through focusing on the mobile phone instead but also human feelings get oppressed and rejected (cf. ibid.). Turkle describes that condition as "a new way of being alone together" (ibid.). Moreover, through the use of social media over a real conversation people have the privilege to perfectly shape and manipulate their post arbitrarily so that mistakes that would happen in real life can be completely avoided and a fake image can be presented to the viewer (cf. ibid.). The vicious circle closes up if the sender himself does not feel listened to and sends more in order to enhance his chances of being listened to but the assumption that the entailed loneliness will decrease through further sending has already been proven as being a fallacy (ibid.).

For Monbiot, the concepts of individualism and competition are striking (cf. Monbiot 10). Aaron can be shown to have already won a certain competition due to him singing "after years with their crown on my head" ("January 1979"). However, he did not care about poorer people but just enjoyed his fame and the things he could afford himself through his fame, which gets clear though a particular line: "*Kept busy indulging in the pleasures of the wealthy*" ("January 1979"). In an interview, Aaron declares that for him now seeing people "trying to look attractive or desirable" is disgusting (Weiss qtdn. E., Tommy). Thus, he describes the rivalry between people in capitalistic states, where individualism is essential for competition on the market but it also seems to favor competition between the people. The singer goes further with his proposition that the mentioned clothing-lifestyle of people "looks [...] like a costume", which means that people are hiding their true selves and are not able to express who they really are any longer (Weiss qtdn. E., Tommy). Instead of that they produce a fake image to fulfill societal demands, which is also depicted as *self-branding* (cf. Khamis et al.). People are sending what society expects them to instead of realizing themselves, as they want to differ from one another to feel special but just in a certain *frame* established by the demands of society, so that lives get *customized* (cf. Turkle). To add a point, Monbiot explains how technology enhances this by referring to the television (cf. Monbiot 11-2). Turkle detects another kind of technology, robots, developed to help people cope with the arising loneliness but simultaneously she refutes the effect of it by finding out that real, enriching communication is not possible with robots (cf. Turkle). The scientist worked out that a robot "can [not] empathize [,] [...] does [not] face death [...] and does [not] know life" (Turkle). She observed a woman talking to a robot that could pretend to listen but not respond, which means that as the woman was sending her inner, individual thoughts to the robot, she did not have a partner who really received (cf. ibid.). This is an extreme example for how the world could look like if it is only sent and the ability of receiving is completely taken away by the human himself.

Since Aaron Weiss sings about "charming [his fans] [...] at best", he means to have said many words showing his affection to his fans but, as it was already worked out, he could not build up a deep relationship to them, so that one could deduce that the primary goal of his words was to feel special through the positive feedback animated by his charming words ("Leaf"). This entailes that he was neither honest with himself nor with his fans. According to Burgoon et al. one could argue that a communication happened between the singer and his fans but it was obviously led by his interests and he was in the power position to cancel the communication any time (cf. Burgoon et al. 21). All in all, Aaron Weiss' fans decoded the charming words as honest compliments, while Aaron primarily had the intention to satisfy his ego. As Aaron expresses the wish for "becom[ing] the servant of all", he demonstrates regret for his actions, including the seduction of his fans ("January 1979"). Hereby, he uses the style of accommodation to cope with his issues because to compensate his one-sided communication with the fans he desires to serve them and thus just to listen to their individual wishes in order to fulfill them (cf. Burgoon et al. 343-4).

Similarly to Aaron Weiss' former approach of gaining reputation, people living in the 21st Century can measure other' and their own value on Social media platforms through "content voting systems, like for instance "*thumbs up* or *thumbs down*" (Kietzmann et al. 247). Therefore, they are under constant pressure to please viewers through producing individual, special, content that distinguishes the producer from all other individuals on Social media platforms (cf. ibid.). During the process, there is more value in creating numerous likes rather than meaningful content, so the individual focusses on a high quantity rather than on the quality of the posts (cf. ibid.). To put it differently: The relationship between the producer and the consumer of a post is not dependent from an underlying deep communication, but from sparking interest on the individual that produced the post and if a communication happens, it is likely that they are "short [and] speedy" because other individuals quickly spark interest to viewers and therefore distract from the former subject (ibid. 244).

Aaron Weiss was perfectly lonely. His instrumentalization of his fans for his own purpose and thus his incapability to build up deep relationships is an indicator that he might have been a greatly lonely person. He has not been able to realize himself alone. When for instance "charming [his fans] at best", he reached for being somehow connected to somebody but as it was already mentioned, he could not build up deep relationships and ended a conversation abruptly if something was led into a direction outside his comfort zone ("Leaf"; cf. Turkle). Through Social media, it is even easier to end up a conversation quickly (cf. Turkle). What can be detected here is that on the one hand, Aaron was dependent on the relationship with his fans and on the other hand, he never managed to meet his fans' expectations and to really appreciate them, which he wants to reconcile later when singing: "If I could become the servant of all" (cf. Turkle; "January 1979").

Through a high amount of Social media- usage, it gets hard for people to concentrate for a longer time on what other people might have to tell them and to process it adequately (cf. Newport). Additionally, it is never guaranteed that the consumed segments of the life of the sender is not manipulated by the sender himself (cf. ibid.). Secondly, due to a lack of concentration and constant pressure to stay informed and to inform about oneself on Social media, people are no longer able to produce something coherent but rather something "that does [not] produce a lot of value" (Newport). Finally, they do not get listened to and become increasingly irrelevant (cf. Newport). Consequences of such circumstances are often mental health issues (cf. ibid.). A well-known mental health issue is loneliness but also depression (cf. ibid.). To move on, it is to mention that the brain gets "[short-circuited]" (ibid.). The next item is that anxiety can develop when not representing oneself on social media in order to recover one's value socially and economically (Newport).

As the 21st Century is described as the "*Age of Loneliness*" by Monbiot, one could already assume that many mental health issues originate from loneliness (Monbiot 9).

Cornwell and Waite explicated that and listed problems like "morbidity and mortality […], as well as infection […], depression […] and cognitive decline" and also "cardiovascular disease [and] inflammation" as arising through loneliness, which can particularly affect older adults in an onerous way due to great changes that happen during that life time (Cornwell and Waite 31-2). Thereby, they distinguished between "[real] social disconnectedness and perceived isolation" (ibid. 33). Especially perceived isolation is strongly correlated to Social media usage where representing oneself and connecting with others plays and important role (cf. Turkle). Individuals feel a lack of support if they are not constantly connecting and by this means ask others to listen to them and appreciate them as individuals (cf. Cornwell and Waite 33; Turkle). Despite that, their relationships with the other people online are rather superficial because people want to keep control (cf. Turkle). That leads to an increased feeling of loneliness and can trigger the mental health issues that were depicted (cf. ibid.).

On Social Media, the term *social* is used to describe the amount of people that build a group, hereby *more people* equals *more social*, which is a fallacy because the quality of these relationships is not payed any attention to but much earlier the quantity (cf. Kietzmann et al. 247; cf. Mortimer 1). It is even evaluated that communities with more than 150 participants, which is the case on most Social media platforms, lead to less "stable social relationships" (Kietzmann et al. 247). That can enhance the problem of loneliness and mental health issues resulting from it. With such high numbers of people it is also likely that these get grouped into subgroups (cf. ibid.). A similar item is the restriction and limits within a group (cf. Kietzmann et al. 248). Overall, these proceedings are called "*filtering*" (ibid.).

Expanding the concept behind the proposition "*I share therefore I am*", meaning that people are sending in order to feel something, one could detect another possible danger: through the personalized filter bubble online one can almost exclusively access subjects that are similar to one's formerly addressed subjects, at least accessing something totally antithetical is less likely through filter bubbles and echo chambers (Turkle; cf. Mortimer 1). The distinction of conspiracy theories and scientific theories gets significantly more difficult through the internet (cf. Mortimer 1). If people become lonely and thus often more narrow-minded, they must, according to logic, automatically become more accessible for conspiracy thinking and radical thinking in general. So, that can be noted as an important consequence of too much focus on oneself too. Another thing that can happen is that people place themselves in radical subgroups that share their specific point of view or ideology (cf. Mortimer 6).

In MewithoutYou's song "January 1979", it is described how someone is "looking down on the tops of the hats of [...] passersby from [the] seventh floor balcony [...] carry[ing] on covert conversation" ("January 1979"). This couple or group of people could symbolize the humans who were talking about the singer Aaron conspiratorially because at Cornerstone Festival 2002 Aaron's "social anxiety, nervous fidgeting, and [other behaviors]" got mistaken for autism which many fans believed since someone expressed that thought (Harrison 47-8). In the song the band makes use of the negatively connoted adjectives "detached [and] vulgar" to draw attention to the problem that comes along with such rumors, but thus also conspiracy theories ("January 1979").

To arrive at a conclusion, all findings from the main part have to be summarized at first, to connect them with the thesis statement from the beginning afterwards.

Firstly, it was noticed that the band mewithoutYou's singer Aaron Weiss personalized the band's music through processing his former self-promoting lifestyle, especially through two particular songs from the album *Catch For Us The Foxes*.

Next, Monbiot's theory for individualism in the 21st Century was explained, whereby the most significant aspect is that people have become and tend to become increasingly lonely due to extreme individualism, enforced through items like language and television that are shaping society.

After that, it was worked out that communication can take different forms and different problems of communication with different outcomes can occur.

During the analysis of the primary sources, it was determined that Weiss was extremely dependent on others in order to live like he desired to and that he took advantage of his family, friends and fans. Similarly to that, it was proven that his behavior is correlated to that of *influencers* on Social media, who want to sell their products and lifestyle to *followers*.

To further prove this as right, it was shown that through the use of Social media people can decide in an individual way where they want to focus their attention to and that their lifestyle is consequently pretty much determined by these decisions.

Last but not least, the consequences of such developments were listed up and explained: People suffer various mental health-issues, especially depression, the focus changes quickly and radicalization of ideologies in subgroups gets easier for individuals.

So, it can be detected that the thesis statement, which contains the idea that communication in the 21st Century became almost impossible due to the focus on sending as a means of expressing one's own individualism, which causes mental and social issues, is valid. People are able to spread various questionable ideologies and ideas, mainly through the help of the internet, and vice versa they can listen to all ideologies and ideas that they want to hear, but if something does not fit their own interests and desires, they can neglect it and instead of listening, focus their attention elsewhere. Thus, an enriching communication, which requires active listeners and contributors, is less likely to happen any longer. This effects the mental health because individuals suffer of constant pressure to promote themselves in order to be listened to and that is then polarizing for society.

Further research has to be conducted when it comes to questionable marketing strategies and radicalization of ideologies that can be spread easily through the internet. Moreover, it is necessary to figure out in how far children are affected by such circumstances of individualism in the 21st Century and how parents can support their children, so that they achieve a higher attention span and get to comprehend what an enriching communication requires.

Works Cited:

Burgoon, Michael, et al. *Human Communication*. Sage Publications, 1994.

Cornwell, Erin York and Linda J. Waite. "Social Disconnectedness, Perceived Isolation, and Health among Older Adults." *Journal of health and social behavior*, vol. 50, no. 1, 2009, pp. 31-48.

E., Tommy. "Mewithoutyou: Short Interview." *Medium*, A Medium Corporation [US], 6 June 2016, medium.com/nefelibata-online/cloud-walkers-mewithoutyou-interview-a5f0a426ecab.

Harrison, Paul Matthew. *all the Clever Words on Pages: a portrait of my friendship with Aaron Weiss of mewithoutYou*. Clever Words, Galena, IL, 2016.

Hall, Stuart. "Encoding/decoding." *Culture, Media, Language*, edited by Stuart Hall,

Dorothy Hobson, Andrew Love, and Paul Willis, London: Hutchinson, 1980, pp. 128-38.

Khamis, Susie, Laurence Ang and Raymond. "Self-branding, 'micro-celebrity' and the rise of Social Media Influencers." *Celebrity Studies*, vol. 8, no. 2, 2016, pp. 191-208.

Kietzmann, Jan H., et al. "Social Media? Get serious! Understanding the functional building blocks of social media." *Business Horizons*, vol. 54, no. 3, 2011, pp. 241-251.

MewithoutYou. Wikipedia. Wikipedia.org, n. p., en.wikipedia.org/wiki/MewithoutYou. Accessed 14 February 2019.

Monbiot, George. *How Did We Get Into This Mess? Politics, Equality, Nature.* Verso, 2016.

Mortimer, Kim. "Understanding Conspiracy Online: Social Media and the Spread of Suspicious Thinking." *Dalhousie Journal of Interdisciplinary Management*, vol. 13, 2017.

Newport, Cal. "Why you should quit social media." *TED*. June 2016. Lecture.

Relevant Magazine. "Interview: Aaron Weiss." *Relevant Magazine*, 5 January 2007, relevantmagazine.com/culture/3472-interview-aaron-weiss/.

Turkle, Sherry. "Connected, but alone?" *TED*. Feb. 2012. Lecture.

Way, Marian. "On Listening." *Clean Language, Quotes*, Clean Learning, 20 July 2014, cleanlearning.co/uk/blog/discuss/on-listening.

Weiss, Aaron. "January 1979." *GENIUS*, Genius Media Group Inc., 15 October 2004, genius.com/Mewithoutyou-january-1979-lyrics.

Weiss, Aaron. "Leaf." *GENIUS*, Genius Media Group Inc., 15 October 2004, genius.com/Mewithoutyou-leaf-lyrics.